Ernst A. Ekker
Doris Eisenburger

W. A. Mozart

A musical picture book

ANNETTE BETZ

"To be in Vienna is the best entertainment!" exclaims Wolfgang Amadé Mozart to Constanze, whom he married just a few weeks ago. "Listen!"

Constanze hears dull pounding, whips cracking, screeching, whistling, and children crying. She stands still and looks down from the city wall. Cattle are being herded towards the gate down there.

Mozart hears something completely different. He grabs his pen and reaches into the coat pocket in which he usually carries some notepaper. With lightning speed he scribbles a melody – and not just the melody! He also jots down the tempo, the rhythm, and the instrumentation needed to bring this tune to life.

"Do you see another opera scene before you?" asks Constanze, smiling.

Mozart nods, "Wild horsemen from the Orient!" Constanze laughs. "Now I understand why you hardly ever stop working and why you even have to write music during a walk on the city wall! All of Vienna is a big stage for you."

Now Mozart laughs, too. "You are correct again. I love this stage – almost as much as I love you. After all, I owe my *new* life to you both."

"Don't you dare love it more than me!" exclaims Constanze. "Then, there would be a stage fight."

A stage fight initiated the beginning of Mozart's *new* life. It began one year ago in 1781 – with a kick!

As a court musician, Wolfgang was staying in Vienna with his lord and "purse-string holder," Archbishop Colloredo of Salzburg.

When Colloredo suddenly decided to return home, the musician refused to follow right away. He had made promising connections on the Viennese music scene, with plans to prepare a concert as well as to compose new works.

His Salzburger lord became angry with the stubborn subordinate. He insulted him, saying "You rascal! Scallywag! Insolent subject! No one has ever served me as poorly as you have! I will take back your salary if you do not return to Salzburg immediately!" Mozart's temper flared up, too. The fight ended with the archbishop firing him. Soon afterwards, Count Karl Josef Arco, the chamberlain in charge of all the musicians and servants of the Salzburg court, evicted 25-year-old Mozart from the room with a kick.

As much as the boastful and beloved musician and composer complained about this treatment, he also breathed easier.

He felt free! He was free to live life as he imagined it – a life with and for his music. And naturally, it was a life with and for Constanze as well. Somehow, he sensed, "This bubbling, clamorous theater city – Vienna – is my city!"

Like Vienna, Salzburg also looks like a stage with magnificent scenery. It is here, in the city of his birth, that Mozart makes his first public appearance. When he is only five years old, he appears in a small comedy – as a *dancer*! Early on, his parents recognize that their Wolferl has music in his blood.

His mother Anna Maria came from a musical family in St. Gilgen, on Lake Wolfgang. She remembers how he began to kick in her womb, as soon as she sang an amusing folk song or hummed a favorite opera melody. He would even kick when her husband Leopold played on his violin, the piano or the organ.

This passion for movement stayed with Wolferl. The rhythm of a piece of music goes to his legs, his hands, and through his whole body.

But, Wolfgang can also sit still and listen dreamily when he hears music. He hears a lot of it in his home at Getreidegasse #9, where he was born on January 27, 1756. After all, his father worked as violinist and assistant Kapellmeister, or director of the court orchestra of Archbishop Schrattenbach, Colloredo's predecessor.

Of course, his father practices at home. He often plays music with his friends. He also

gives piano lessons to his daughter Nannerl, who is four and a half years older than Wolferl. It is no wonder then, that the boy of only three years old begs to be allowed to also learn to play the piano – and the violin, and the viola, and the organ…

As the parents soon note with amazement, a miraculous ability emerges in the boy. After only a short time, Wolferl plays the piano as well as his talented sister. After listening to them only once, he replays melodies right away. He can even play melodies that have *never been heard before*! His fingers magically call forth from the instrument notes which exist only in his mind.

Sometimes he practices a piece of music, experimenting with it until it becomes something completely different, something new. He has no idea that his father Leopold is thinking, "There is *money* to be made with this prodigy. Maybe lots of money." This is a game for Wolferl, something he finds fun. It's just like this dance he is learning for his own amusement right now. It's for the stage performance, and he practices everywhere. He becomes enraptured and wild – especially when his parents and Nannerl are watching – at home in the garden, behind the house, on the cathedral steps or around a burbling city fountain.

Father Leopold regards his family's miracle as a gift from God. He does not want to hide it at home. "The whole world should see and hear it. People will be ceaselessly amazed. And to think that this is happening in an age when the scholars claim to be able to explain everything."

He is already scheming: "We have to take concert tours with Wolferl." Father Leopold becomes a perfect manager. He knows that guest performances must be well prepared. Nothing can be left to chance. He also knows that less can go wrong with two child prodigies than with one. Therefore, he prepares a "Wolferl and Nannerl" program. He mails letters to influential friends and acquaintances in the cities where concerts are planned. Flyers with reports of the children's wonderful piano playing are sent to the newspapers. He even takes out paid advertisements. It is clear to him that creative promotion is only half the battle. The court musician Leopold Mozart must take additional vacation time for each tour. He invests lots of money in the undertaking. The money he borrows from business people in Salzburg is spent on postal coach rides, for room and board in guesthouses, for clothing and for wigs. He buys a travel piano so that they can practice on the way, and which they also need for guesthouse concerts.

An experienced courtier, Leopold knows that the invitations of kings, princes or counts often bring only fame and honor. The big money is made at public events – with paid admissions.

No matter how carefully Leopold plans each trip, mishaps always occur. There is trouble even when he buys his own coach for the family so that they may travel more comfortably. On one trip when Wolferl is seven, mother Anna Maria comes along because the children often become sick. Furthermore, it is supposed to be a long trip through Germany, to France and then England. Even before their first stop at Wasserburg am Inn, a wheel breaks.

How good that mother insisted that their young servant Sebastian comes along! With his persistence, he scrounges up a replacement wheel. It is smaller than the other three wheels, but so what! Wolferl will never forget this "crooked ride" to the next coach stop. Nor will Sebastian, who is a trained Figaro (barber). This helpful, cheerful servant lives on today in one of the most beloved Mozart operas, *The Marriage of Figaro*.

England is near, but far from sight. Eight-year-old Wolferl "expertly" inspects the boat on the crossing to Calais. After all, he traveled with his father and sister on a Danube boat from Passau to Linz and on to Vienna only two years ago.

It doesn't take long before he befriends the crew. A British sailor says, "Good morning, sir! How do you do?" He is amazed when Wolferl fires back in English, "Very well, sir, at your service!"

The boy from Salzburg, who does not go to school – and never will – has learned not only Italian and French from his father, but already knows a few words of English too.

His mother worries about him, "Don't walk around so much on the boat; you'll become seasick." Then, she is the first one to become ill from this unpredictable ailment.

As sympathetic as Wolferl is, he has to laugh when she – and soon thereafter, the others – hang over the railing.

The laughter suddenly sticks in his throat. There! Is that not a monster rising from the fog? It trumpets and trumpets, so that Wolferl must hold his ears shut with his hands. It's like at home, when trumpeter Schachtner comes to visit. The boat rocks more and more. The ocean rumbles and grumbles.

The fog elephant disappears. Still, the trumpeting can be heard. Is it a storm? A foghorn?

"You are insulting my ears!" scolds Wolferl.

Originally, he had looked forward to the promised family visit to the London Zoo. Now, he doesn't feel like going anymore. The animals there are supposed to be quite loud…

To distract himself, he wants to think about something funny. He remembers a few months ago at the New Year's celebration at the French royal court in Versailles. As a special favor, selected guests of the royal family are allowed to watch the meal. Nonetheless, Wolferl is allowed to stand next to the dining queen, and to kiss her hand now and then. Once, she even graciously lets him take a bite of her roasted chicken. He almost kisses her chicke and bites her hand!

But later, for "dessert," he is permitted to play the piano for the royal family. He plays a duet with Nannerl, all four hands together. He is allowed to present his first *published* compositions, brand new pieces for violin and piano.

His memories are suddenly interrupted. "I shouldn't have thought about eating," he groans as he too leans over the railing.

The heavens smile again, little by little," sighs mother Anna Maria with relief. Wolferl asks for a pen. He wants to compose more – starting where he left off a few weeks ago, due to severe illness. Now he is too weak. Therefore, his mother supports his hand as he writes the score for the new violin sonata.

The family stays much longer here in The Hague than they had planned. First Nannerl lay at death's door with typhoid fever, and then her brother. Their father sees the money they have earned on this world tour, especially during the one and a half years in England, dwindling away. To the boy, it seems that his mother never left his bedside. He saw her face and felt her hand stroking him or wiping the sweat from his brow whenever he startled awake from his feverish dreams. During lucid moments he heard her humming songs from Salzburg or little melodies which he, himself had composed.

He was so tired that he would have preferred not to wake up anymore. Still, she tried to make him laugh with her cheerful voice, "Do you remember how the people insisted on having autographed pictures of the child prodigies last year? And father said: *Too expensive!* And you said: *Well, then let us make a whole bunch and sell them!* And then father's befuddled face when the pictures sold like hot cakes!…"

"Do you remember the mistrustful scientist in London who thought you were a trained monkey? How he observed you! But you paid no attention to him as you let your ideas flow out of the piano as always – until he finally exclaimed: *Amazing! This child is a natural!* Then he nearly fell unconscious – and you simply crouched on the floor and petted his cat…"

"Do you remember how excited father was about the English concert promoters? With their advertising, they succeeded in selling out the halls before we even set foot in London. Our stunned father: *A concert here brings in more than I earn during a year in Salzburg!*"

One day Wolferl says, almost inaudibly, "Do you remember, in London, how all four of us walked to the church as often as possible, and how our friends thought we were especially pious? Really, I only wanted to practice the organ!"

Now mother Anna Maria knows that Wolferl is on the mend. She smiles, "Do you remember how you hopped up and down on the organ during the concert for the royal family? And how the queen remarked: *The little one is the best organist I know!*" Wolferl tries to laugh. "She probably doesn't know many organists."

Father Leopold travels with his family to Vienna for a big wedding. Maria Theresia's 16-year-old daughter is to marry the King of Naples. "And where there is marriage, there are festivities. We will be needed. Maybe Wolferl will be allowed to compose something for the bride and groom."

But then everything changes as a smallpox epidemic breaks out in Vienna. The bride dies from the menacing disease.

The Mozart family flees to friends in Olomouc. It doesn't help. Soon after arriving, Wolferl is stricken with smallpox. A little later, so is Nannerl.

Mother Anna Maria has to be a nurse again. The night shift wears her out so much that she loses about 20 pounds. Father Leopold helps her during the day sometimes when he does not have pressing errands to accomplish.

Unlike the Emperor's family, the Mozart family is lucky and both children survive.

Father Leopold already praises the new "miracle" wherever he goes. He proclaims, "God has *big* things in store for our son. That is why he was spared."

Many people say that such statements are boastful. Others sense a clever advertising gag behind them.

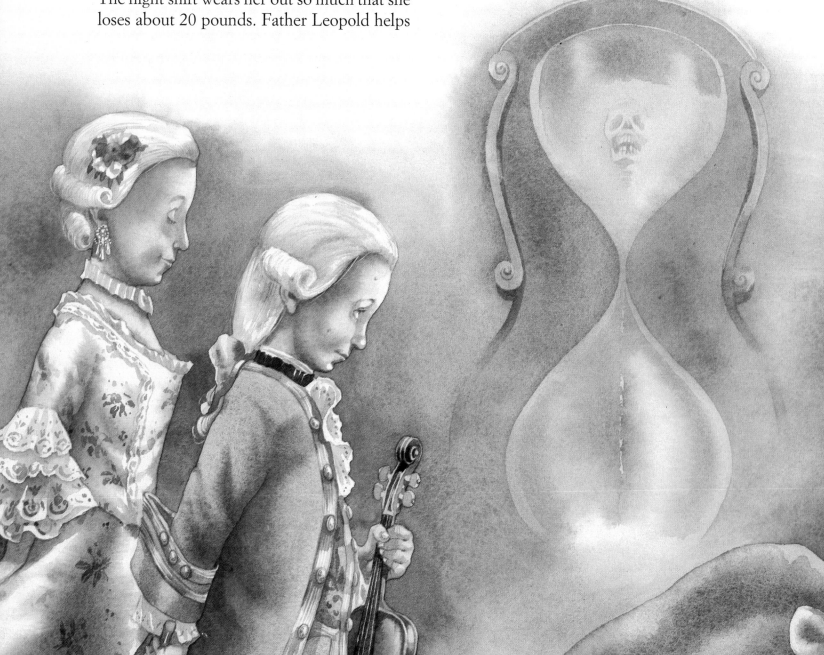

Father Leopold probably hopes the new miracle will bring an imperial commission for his son. Word travels quickly in Vienna.

When the Mozart family is admitted to the mourning audience, Wolferl feels an ice-cold breeze. The empress sits there like a stone. No sooner than father has mumbled his condolences, he is dismissed.

Then Maria Theresia looks at mother Anna Maria. The empress pauses and waves her over.

Suddenly, the boy has a lump in his throat. There his mother stands, and looks at the other mother. She doesn't need to say a word – the other one understands her and gently strokes her cheek.

Still, from now on father Leopold will demand *even more* from his son, the "gift from God." He will never be satisfied with what prodigy Wolferl does.

He fears, "We are in a race for time." What he means is: "Who knows how long the prodigy's name will be famous."

He is right about the race, but in a completely different sense. His son will die at the young age of 35. Despite this, one will know his name – and his music – even centuries later.

Cara sorella mia! My dear sister! Today Vesuvius is smoking heavily. *Wow!* Wolferl takes a walk though the streets of the old Roman city Pompeii with his father. It was "extinguished" under the volcano's lava and just recently excavated. The Pompeiian ruins are like giant stage scenery to him. And the smoke from Vesuvius turns into comedy masks.

Wolferl has wanted to write an opera since hearing his first big one at the age of six during Munich's carnival. At a young age, he starts to compose arias, songs for singers he has met on his many travels. They scramble to have a composition dedicated to them by the world-famous child prodigy. What he would really like to do is to compose an opera sung only by children.

Again and again, he attends opera performances on his tours across Europe. He loves the serious, ceremonial court music spectacle (Opera seria) as much as musical comedy (Opera buffa). To understand the secret of opera, he studies all the scores (the books in which the notes of all of the voice and instrument parts are written out). He also studies many librettos (the books containing the words or texts of operas).

Italy is the land of opera. Italian operas are performed all over the world – in Vienna and Munich, just as in Paris and London. The best places of course, are Milan, Venice, Naples, and Florence.

So, father Leopold and his son travel to Italy. They go there many times, for long trips. Nannerl is hurt because she isn't allowed to come along. But, she is no longer a child prodigy, she is a young woman of 18 years. As consolation, her brother writes her funny letters:

Yesterday, we went to the opera in Naples. The theater is beautiful. The king is rudely Neapolitan. At the opera, he always stands on a stool so that he appears a tiny bit taller than the queen. The queen is pretty and polite, and must have greeted me in the most friendly way at least six times.

Wolferl doesn't attract mass audiences any more either. Who still wonders about a 14-year-old who has played his "masterpieces" all over the world for so many years now?

Still, this Wolfgang Amadeo (as he calls himself in Italy) remains a wonder, as a composer. But, only a few people realize this – such as the well-known composer Joseph Haydn.

Father Leopold would like his son to realize his fortune in Italy, just like Johann Christian Bach (Johann Sebastian Bach's youngest son). This German is beloved in England as an "Italian" composer.

Sure enough, father Leopold's plan appears to work. In short order, the name Mozart is known in Italian musical circles. Now his music is acclaimed, just as the child prodigy had been in times past.

The best Italian players perform his instrumental music. Three of his operas are premiered in Milan – successfully.

Still, none of this leads to spectacular consequences. The operas are not performed in other theaters and the successes die out quickly.

The time in Italy is a *flop* for father Leopold because the big money stays away. He puzzles, "Why does everything go wrong?"

Mozart, the young musician, soon feels cramped in Salzburg. "There's not even an opera house here," he complains.

Since he was 14, Wolfgang has worked as concertmaster at the Archbishop's court. He was not even paid for the first three years. His father works for the spiritual prince as well. He is the court composer, whose salary does not stretch far. Nonetheless, father and son receive generous vacations for their many long journeys. This suddenly ends. Colloredo forbids another tour. Maybe he suspects what father Leopold has planned: His now 21-year-old son shall apply for a well-paid position as court composer for another prince. He could go to Munich, or Mannheim (which has the best orchestra in all of Europe right now), or

maybe even to Paris! "The young queen of France knows you, Wolferl. She is Marie Antoinette, with whom you played in Vienna at the emperor's court. Audition for her. She is self-confident, but not arrogant."

So it is that Wolfgang looks for work in Munich, Mannheim, and Paris. But no one seems to need a new court composer. He is not even admitted to see Marie Antoinette.

Wolfgang is not too unhappy over this. He uses the time to compose. He also uses it to meet young people. He is "hungry" for people, for friends.

When Wolfgang hears that Johann Christian Bach is staying in Paris, he visits him – and is disappointed. Fourteen years ago in London, Johann chatted much more affectionate-

ly with him, and gave him tips on composing…

Wolfgang receives an even larger shock when he is supposed to give a concert at the home of a Parisian count. He has to wait a long time, the salon is unheated, and the piano is out-of-tune. Finally, the lady of the house appears with her guests. She laughs amusedly when he complains of not being used to such treatment. Then, she gives him a sign to start playing. Mozart begins to perform and loses himself in his world of sound. As he glances up, he freezes: the audience has spread out enormous sketchpads, and is drawing! No one is paying attention to him. No one is listening to the unusual music. The young composer realizes, "I am playing for the chairs and for the walls!" He springs up angrily and wants to leave the room. And then he suddenly sees the audience as it *really* is. And, he has to laugh. And in a way, he feels sorry for them. He sits down and continues playing. "Maybe the chairs and the walls are *listening*."

Soon thereafter, he returns to the service of the Archbishop in Salzburg, where he will remain for a number of years. His father called him back, as he perceives Wolfgang to be "incapable." Though his son composed immortal works during this trip such as the *Parisian Symphony*, it is something he doesn't want to recognize.

Mozart has an extraordinary dream: he sees a life thread, *his* life thread. And he sees people on whose laps he is gleefully hopping.

"What? I hopped on so many people's laps?" he wonders.

There is his mother, whose life was in danger at his birth. She bore seven children in eight years but only Nannerl and he survived. Still, she sings jauntily,

"Good day, good day, Spitzignas!
Knallerballer! Who is that?
Bagatellerl. Bagatollferl. It's Wolferl!"

And as long as she sings, he cannot get down. Yet at the same time, he sits on his father's knees! What others learned in school, he learned from his father – and much more, especially composing.

Of course, after some time Wolferl wants to hop off and play. But his father holds him tight by saying all of his names – like casting a spell: "Johannes Chrysostomus Wolfgangus Theophilus! Theophilus: Amadeo Amadé Amadeus! Loved by God, loved by God!"

Empress Maria Theresia doesn't let him off of her lap either, and pats him as though he were her child. With a silky voice, she coos,

"Schlumba tumbla ks ks ks!
Stri-o stru-o bs bs bs!"

First he enjoys this, and then he thinks, "Over time, even the most beautiful imperial voice can get on your nerves!" In the same moment, the voice is transformed into princely garments, which fit Wolferl like a glove. As much as he tries, he can't get out of the clothes, which actually belong to Max, the empress's youngest son.

Luckily, he now sits on Johann Christian Bach's lap in front of a grand piano. Twenty fingers race over the keys. And the keys jubilate.

Because Bach's fingers can't stop as they continuously conjure up new melodies from the instrument, Mozart's fingers can't rest either. They immediately find the notes to accompany the Bach piece. "Listen my lungs, my liver, my stomach, too; look at what we dare to do!"

Suddenly Mozart is horrified, "Have we not already played all of this? No, not once, but often! I do not want to have to hear the same thing forever!"

Prince Colloredo's voice thunders threateningly in his ears. And Mozart thinks, "I do not want to have *to do* the same thing forever!"

He inhales deeply and prepares to jump. Already, he is high above the mighty, princely shadow and over the magnificent city of Salzburg, which takes his breath away. He goes past his father, who is about to spread his arms to catch him.

"Hey they say
Say they hey
the child prodigy hops away," rejoices Mozart.

He would love to see the following scenes, but his life thread is lost in a fog. Mozart ponders, "O, that I would be! If God wanted, I would be! I became! I become!…"

"What are you mumbling?" the voice of his wife Constanze penetrates his thoughts.

"I *am*!" says Mozart and wakes up.

"What?" asks Constanze.

"I am *yours*," he laughs. And he showers her with kisses.

There is much dancing in Vienna – especially during carnival. Wolfgang Amadé likes to dance boisterously, often into the early morning hours. Constanze is an enthusiastic dancer, too.

He finally has friends here in Vienna, and he needs them like his daily bread. After working, he is often burned out. He doesn't write mechanically, strictly following the composition rules he mastered long ago. He shapes what he learned into something new, which flows out from within him. He views this particular unexplainable ability as a gift from God. But, this also drains his energy. It is no wonder that after completing a large work, Mozart often throws himself into "complete pleasure." He goes to the theater, to masked balls, and has conversations with people who are close to him as well as with strangers. Many of these experiences later flow back into his works – especially into his operas.

In any case, his first attempt at taking root in Vienna is successful. Mozart even lives in grand style, with an expensive city apartment and servants – despite being unemployed, working only as a freelance composer for a variety of clients.

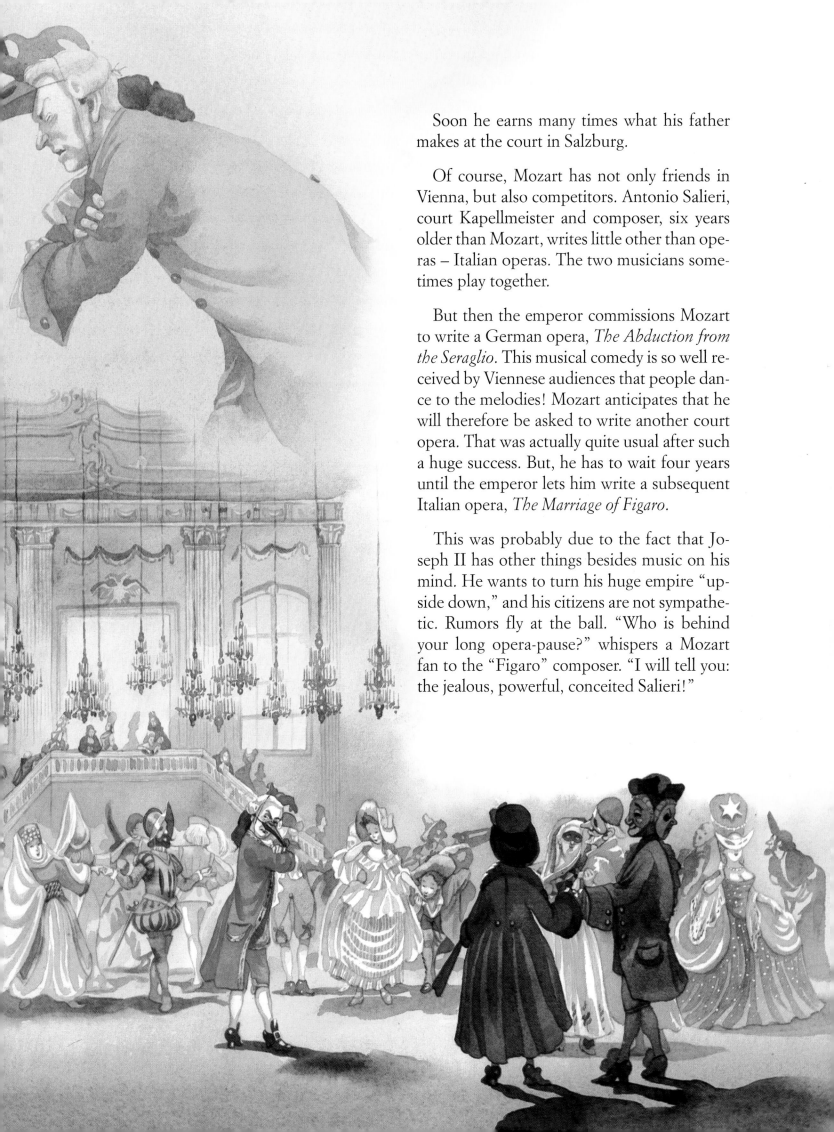

Soon he earns many times what his father makes at the court in Salzburg.

Of course, Mozart has not only friends in Vienna, but also competitors. Antonio Salieri, court Kapellmeister and composer, six years older than Mozart, writes little other than operas – Italian operas. The two musicians sometimes play together.

But then the emperor commissions Mozart to write a German opera, *The Abduction from the Seraglio*. This musical comedy is so well received by Viennese audiences that people dance to the melodies! Mozart anticipates that he will therefore be asked to write another court opera. That was actually quite usual after such a huge success. But, he has to wait four years until the emperor lets him write a subsequent Italian opera, *The Marriage of Figaro*.

This was probably due to the fact that Joseph II has other things besides music on his mind. He wants to turn his huge empire "upside down," and his citizens are not sympathetic. Rumors fly at the ball. "Who is behind your long opera-pause?" whispers a Mozart fan to the "Figaro" composer. "I will tell you: the jealous, powerful, conceited Salieri!"

Mozart knows, "I only need to hear talk of an opera, I need only be in the theater before I hear voices – and already, I am beside myself!"

How "beside himself" must he be with respect to his own operas. Wolfgang Amadé is a born musical theater man. He not only thinks in music, but also in pictures. He sees the scenes unfold, even while he is still composing them. Heaven forbid when the rehearsals don't run just the way he has imagined them. On occasion he would jump from the stage into the orchestra pit to yank the instrument from the hands of a violinist who has played incorrectly, and demonstrate the passage in the way it is supposed to sound. In Prague's Stände Theater, he wrings his hands in despair. His *Don Giovanni* is being rehearsed. The singer in the role of Donna Elvira stares unemotionally at the monument to the dead commander – even though the stone statue becomes alive.

"Please *cry out* in horror!" advises Mozart. "I cannot scream. I can only sing."

"Nonsense! Everyone can scream, especially when one is frightened," insists Mozart. The scene is repeated. The singer stands there in silence. At the next run-through, Mozart sneaks behind "Elvira" unnoticed and pinches her. She winces and screams. Mozart is delighted, "Superb!"

Many singers and musicians cannot stand Mozart because he demands nearly as much dedication from them as he does from himself. His wife Constanze is familiar with his habit of intense absorption, as she experiences the situation often enough. Wolfgang throws himself into his work with such concentration that he forgets everything around him. As a child, every sound, even that of the most beautiful trumpet-playing, bothered him and hurt his ears. Now, luckily he can compose in the midst of the biggest commotion of a guesthouse. He can even work in the ruckus of his large Viennese city apartment when the servants argue, his youngest child bawls, a composition student hammers at the piano, a voice student sings shrilly, and Constanze tells him something important, all at once.

Mozart works, but no one sees it. He merely stands there or walks back and forth. The most artistic compositions develop in his *head*. He conceives not only the melodies, but all of the complicated and surprising details of the score! Then when he puts the newly "born" music on paper, he writes with lightning speed. Meanwhile, he can still listen to Constanze and hold a conversation with her. Not even the shrilly screaming student can disrupt his newest creation.

The people of Prague have taken Mozart and his music into their hearts. They are much more devoted than the Viennese audiences, which stagger from one sensation to the next (as many critics claim). Not only has Mozart numerous singers to thank for the fact that all of Prague is stricken with Mozart-fever and that many people know *The Abduction* and *Figaro* almost by heart. He must also give credit to a *real* Figaro: the Mozart family's former servant, Sebastian. He has worked for Prince Fürstenberg in Donaueschingen for a long time and he has promoted Mozart's name at this court. Now, one of Fürstenberg's daughters lives in Prague. It is her musical valet – a friend of Sebastian's – who proclaims the Viennese composer from Salzburg.

Once again, a travel coach awaits Mozart at the break of dawn. His wife, friends and his dog, Gauckerl, are already sitting inside in good spirits. "Away, away to Prague! To your favorite city!" exclaims Constanze. Wolfgang Amadé stands like a statue on the street. "He is composing again," she thinks. Then she is frightened as a sinister figure has appeared behind her husband. Wolfgang Amadé flinches too, as he suddenly feels a hand on his shoulder. He spins around, and for a moment he thinks he's seen the Grim Reaper before him, calling him on his final journey. But then he has to laugh at himself. He recognizes the messenger, and knows immediately what he wants. His name is Leitgeb, and he is the steward of Count Walsegg-Stuppach, from the Gloggnitz region. A few weeks ago, the Count requested that Mozart write him a Requiem (a Mass for the dead). He has already sent a payment, and a curious contract. Mozart is to receive another considerable sum when he delivers the finished work. But he must provide the original, from which he may not make any copies.

Is the Count a collector of famous handwriting? Or does he want to pass off the Requiem as his own composition? Regardless, Mozart wants to honor the contract, as he needs the money. However, he must put off the messenger, for the Requiem is not even half finished.

In the coach, Wolfgang Amadé sits very still, as though lost in dismal thought. Constanze fears that the sinister stranger has taken his travel lust. She attempts to cheer him up. Their friends join in, sharing the latest gossip about Emperor Joseph II. But Mozart continues to compose the "Last Judgment" (Dies irae) for the Requiem. Somehow, he feels blocked towards this "Day of wrath, punishment, and tears." He doesn't perceive death as frightening, but as a friend who brings rest and who leads people towards the light.

The music in Mozart's head is drowned out by his traveling companions' voices, "And so Countess Pallavicini meets Countess Kinsky, speaking so loudly that the Emperor behind her overhears: *Poor us, Dearest! Our highness, his Majesty, gives the common folk the Prater and the Augarten, and possibly also the park at Schönbrunn! For us, there is no little spot in which we can hang out among our equals, undisturbed!*"

"At this, the Emperor turns around, saying: *If I want to be undisturbed among my equals, then I have to take a walk in the Capuchin crypt.*"

Mozart breaks out in peals of laughter – without even becoming angry that the "Last Judgement" is suddenly whisked from his mind. "The music will come back when the time is right," he tells himself.

I am entirely in my music," claims Mozart. Because of this, some find him pretentious. Yet when he is 31, Joseph II honors him with the title "Imperial-Royal Chamber Composer." He now has the position father Leopold dreamed of for him for so many years. Sadly, his father has recently died before realizing his dream.

Despite his title and the fixed salary, Wolfgang Amadé is still allowed to freelance. The only requirement is that he delivers dance music in time for the imperial masked festivals. Soon, people will dance to melodies from Mozart operas again, this time from *The Magic Flute*. Theater director and comedian Emanuel Schikaneder has requested the opera for his stage, and has written the libretto himself. The fairy tale of the comical bird catcher Papageno and the helpless Prince Tamino who is afraid of monsters, but who wants to free an abducted princess, is a big hit with audiences and quickly becomes a lasting success. Maybe it's only because this opera is full of surprises. Whether it is the "Queen of the Night," the abductor Sarastro, or the colorful crone Papagena, they are all not what they first appear to be to either the Prince or Papageno – and thus, to the audience. Little by little, the Prince loses his prejudices, and *together* with Princess Pamina he faces difficult trials. They persevere, and vow to create a *better world* – a world free of hate and violence, but which is not at all boring because love makes life far more colorful. Even Papageno learned this lesson through his Papagena.

Mozart senses that he has achieved something extraordinary with *The Magic Flute*: "a middle ground between too challenging and too simplistic. Brilliant music, pleasing to the ears, without missing the mark."

During his lifetime, people thought Mozart could be played like a puppet: his father, Archbishop Colloredo and other patriarchs, theater directors, musicians, singers, and prima donnas.

Mozart lives on, over 200 years after his death. After all, he is entirely in his music. The versatility of Amadeus (as he is known today) is amazing. No other composer is "at home" in so many musical genres: symphonies, chamber music, sacred music, solo music, songs and opera. His *Magic Flute* is the most frequently performed opera in the world. Mozart calls the shots with respect to his compositions – sometimes strictly, sometimes lovingly. He tosses a challenge to the conductors, the musicians and the directors. They constantly discover something new in his music. Still, it remains full of secrets. And Mozart laughs.

After you have traveled through time with Wolfgang Amadé Mozart and have visited his world, we suggest: Take your time looking at the pictures while sampling some of Mozart's music. The CD on the next page was specifically selected for this picture book.

IN VIENNA

1. The Abduction from the Seraglio, Overture (excerpt), K. 384
   Capella Istropolitana, Conductor Barry Wordsworth
   Naxos CD 8.550185
   © + ℗ 1989 HNH International Ltd.

THE DANCER

2. German Dance No. 3 (Three German Dances for Orchestra, K. 605)
   Capella Istropolitana, Conductor Johannes Wildner
   Naxos CD 8.550412
   © + ℗ 1990 HNH International Ltd.

FIGARO SEBASTIAN

3. "Non più andrai," Figaro's Aria from The Marriage of Figaro, K. 492
   Andrea Martin, baritone; Vienna Mozart Orchestra, Conductor Konrad Leitner
   Naxos CD 8.550867
   © 1993 HNH International Ltd.
   ℗ 1990 HNH International Ltd.

THE JOURNEY TO ENGLAND

4. The Marriage of Figaro, Overture, K. 492
   Capella Istropolitana, Conductor Barry Wordsworth
   Naxos CD 8.550185
   © + ℗ 1989 HNH International Ltd.

ILL IN THE HAGUE

5. Sonata for Piano in G Major, 2nd Movement Andante, K. 283 (excerpt)
   Jenö Jandó, piano
   Naxos CD 8.550447
   © + ℗ 1991 HNH International Ltd.

6. Twelve Variations on "Ah, je vous dirai, maman" for Organ, K. 265 (excerpt)
   Janós Sebestyén, organ
   Naxos CD 8.550514
   © + ℗ 1991 HNH International Ltd.

THE TWO MOTHERS

7. Mass in C Major ("Coronation Mass"), Ave Verum, K. 317
   Camerata Cassovia, Conductor Johannes Wildner
   Naxos CD 8.550495
   © + ℗ 1991 HNH International Ltd.

THE RUINS OF POMPEII

8. "Deh, vieni alla finestra", Don Giovanni's Aria from Don Giovanni, K. 527
   Andrea Martin, baritone; Vienna Mozart Orchestra, Conductor Konrad Leitner
   Naxos CD 8.550435
   © 1991 HNH International Ltd.
   ℗ 1990 HNH International Ltd.

CONCERT IN PARIS

9. Sonata for Piano in C Major, 1st Movement Allegro, K. 279 (excerpt)
   Jenö Jandó, piano
   Naxos CD 8.550447
   © + ℗ 1991 HNH International Ltd.

THE LIFE THREAD

10. A Little Nightmusic, 1st Movement Allegro, K. 525 (excerpt)
    Capella Istropolitana, Conductor Wolfgang Sobotka
    Naxos CD 8.550026
    © 1991 HNH International Ltd.
    ℗ 1989 HNH International Ltd.

THE SQUABBLERS

11. Sonata for Piano in A-Major "Alla Turca" (arranged for orchestra), K. 331
    Vienna Mozart Orchestra, Conductor Konrad Leitner
    Naxos CD 8.550866
    © 1993 HNH International Ltd.
    ℗ 1990 HNH International Ltd.

OPERA IN PRAGUE

12. Don Giovanni, Overture, K. 527
    Capella Istropolitana, Conductor Barry Wordsworth
    Naxos CD 8.550185
    © + ℗ HNH International Ltd.

THE SINISTER MESSENGER

13. Requiem, Dies Irae, K. 626
    choir and orchestra of the Slovak Philharmonic, Conductor Zdeněk Košler
    Naxos CD 8.550235
    © 1991 HNH International Ltd.
    ℗ 1986 Opus Records

THE PUPPETEER

14. "Wie stark ist nicht dein Zauberton," Tamino's Aria from The Magic Flute, K. 620
    Herbert Lippert, tenor, Failoni Orchestra, Conductor Michael Halász
    Naxos CD 8.660030
    © + ℗ 1994 HNH International Ltd.

15. "Der Vogelfänger bin ich ja," Papageno's Aria from The Magic Flute, K. 620
    Georg Tichy, baritone, Failoni Orchestra, Conductor Michael Halász
    Naxos CD 8.660030
    © + ℗ 1994 HNH International Ltd.

16. "Pa-Pa-Pa," Papageno/Papagena Duet from The Magic Flute
    Georg Tichy, baritone, Lotte Leitner, soprano; Failoni Orchestra, Conductor Michael Halász
    Naxos CD 8.660031
    © + ℗ 1994 HNH International Ltd.